WHO MADE MY LUNCH?

FROM WHEAT TO PASTA

BY MARI SCHUH · ILLUSTRATED BY JEANINE MURCH

AMICUS ILLUSTRATED
is published by Amicus Learning, an imprint of Amicus
P.O. Box 227, Mankato, MN 56002
www.amicuspublishing.us

LIBRARY OF CONGRESS CATALOGING-IN-PUBLICATION DATA
Names: Schuh, Mari C., 1975- author. | Murch, Jeanine Henderson, illustrator.
Title: From wheat to pasta / by Mari Schuh ; illustrated by Jeanine Murch.
Description: Mankato, MN : Amicus Illustrated is published by Amicus Learning, an imprint of Amicus, [2025] | Series: Who made my lunch? | Includes bibliographical references. | Audience: Ages 6-9 | Audience: Grades 2-3 | Summary: "A child wonders where pasta comes from and learns about the jobs of a wheat farmer, a miller, and pasta factory workers as they describe the steps in making pasta. This illustrated narrative nonfiction book includes a world map of where wheat is grown, glossary, and further resources, making it a great story to support farm-to-table education"— Provided by publisher.
Identifiers: LCCN 2024010614 (print) | LCCN 2024010615 (ebook) | ISBN 9798892001120 (library binding) | ISBN 9798892001700 (paperback) | ISBN 9798892002288 (ebook)
Subjects: LCSH: Pasta products—Juvenile literature. | Wheat—Harvesting—Juvenile literature.
Classification: LCC TP435.M3 S38 2025 (print) | LCC TP435.M3 (ebook) | DDC 664/.755—dc23/eng/20240409
LC record available at https://lccn.loc.gov/2024010614
LC ebook record available at https://lccn.loc.gov/2024010615

EDITOR: Rebecca Glaser
SERIES DESIGNER: Kathleen Petelinsek
BOOK DESIGNER: Kim Pfeffer

Printed in China

FOR HARPER AND LILLY—M.S.

ABOUT THE AUTHOR

Mari Schuh's love of reading began with cereal boxes at the kitchen table. Today she is the author of hundreds of nonfiction books for beginning readers. She lives in the Midwest with her husband and their sassy house rabbit. Mari's favorite pasta is spaghetti.

ABOUT THE ILLUSTRATOR

Jeanine Murch is an illustrator with a lifelong love of art, books, and storytelling. She lives in Pittsburgh, PA, with her husband, two children, and the world's most snuggly pup, all of which inspire her work. When she isn't making art, she's usually daydreaming about her next travel adventure.

Pasta is often a yummy part of a healthy lunch. But what if you had to make the pasta from scratch? And grow the wheat yourself?

Start your tractor! You're now a farmer in North Dakota. In the spring, plant durum wheat seeds. This wheat has a lot of protein. It is used to make pasta.

Durum wheat grows well in North Dakota and Canada. These places have cool nights and hot, dry days.

The wheat grows all spring and summer. The stems grow tall. Spikes form. They hold flowers that make wheat kernels.

By September, your field is full of beautiful amber wheat. It is harvest time here in North Dakota. Drive a combine to get the job done. The combine cuts and sorts the wheat. It puts kernels in the hopper. It puts other plant parts on the field.

Next stop—the grain elevator. First, workers weigh your wheat.

Then they load the wheat into tall silos, where it will stay until it's milled.

At the mill, machines blow air to get rid of dust and dirt. They get rid of stones and broken wheat, too.

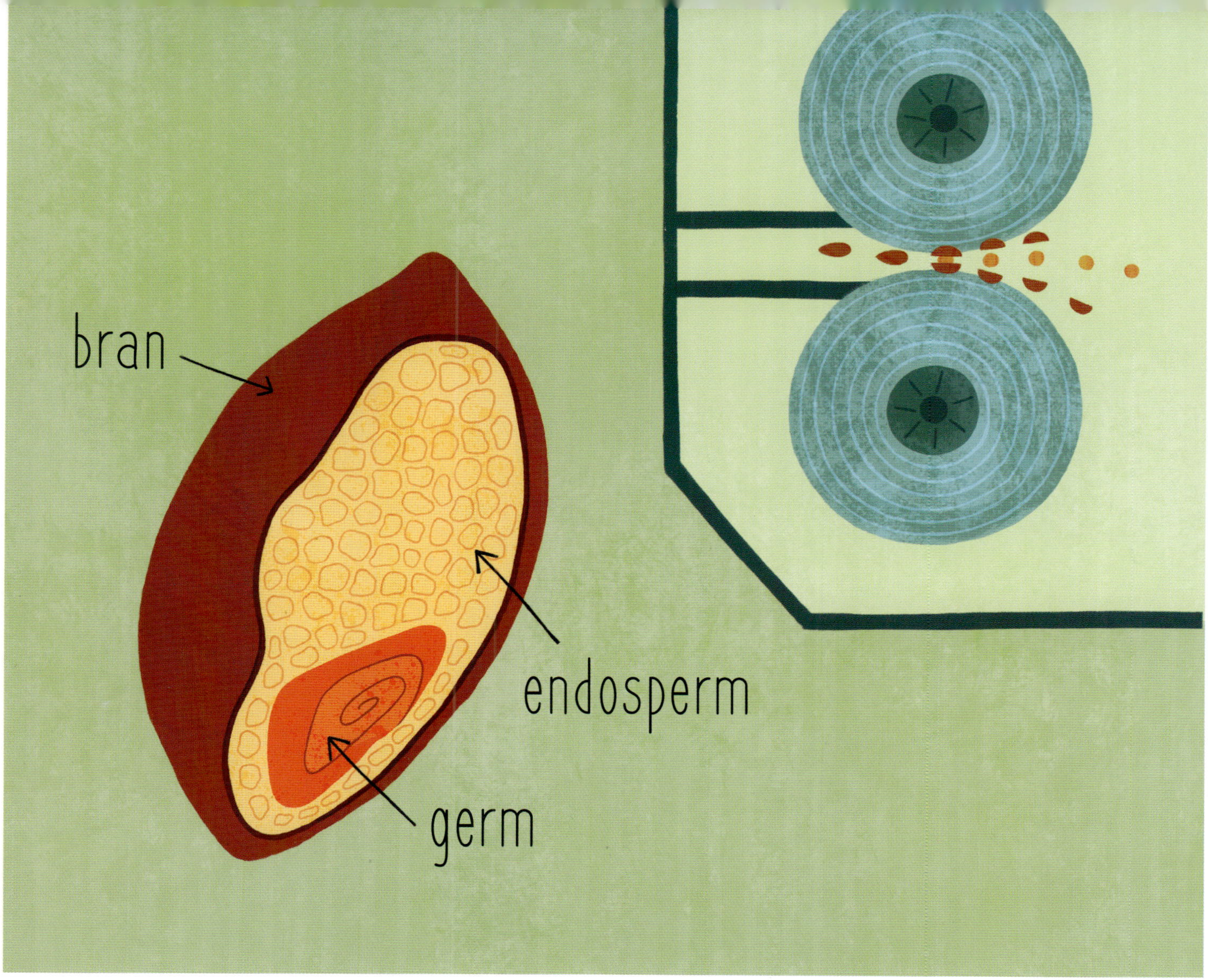

Wheat kernels have three parts: the bran, germ, and endosperm. Rollers separate these parts. Then machines grind the endosperm. They grind and sift, again and again.

Finally, you have semolina flour. It feels rough and coarse. The texture is perfect for making pasta.

Workers test the flour and check its texture and its yellow color.

Now the flour goes to the pasta factory.

At the factory, it's time to mix. A strong machine mixes the semolina with warm water.

Soon, you have dough. Machines knead the dough. Rolling pins press it into sheets.

Then the dough moves to the extruder. Squeeeze! It pushes the dough through metal discs with holes. Different shaped holes make different pasta shapes. Sharp blades cut some pasta. Now it's the right length.

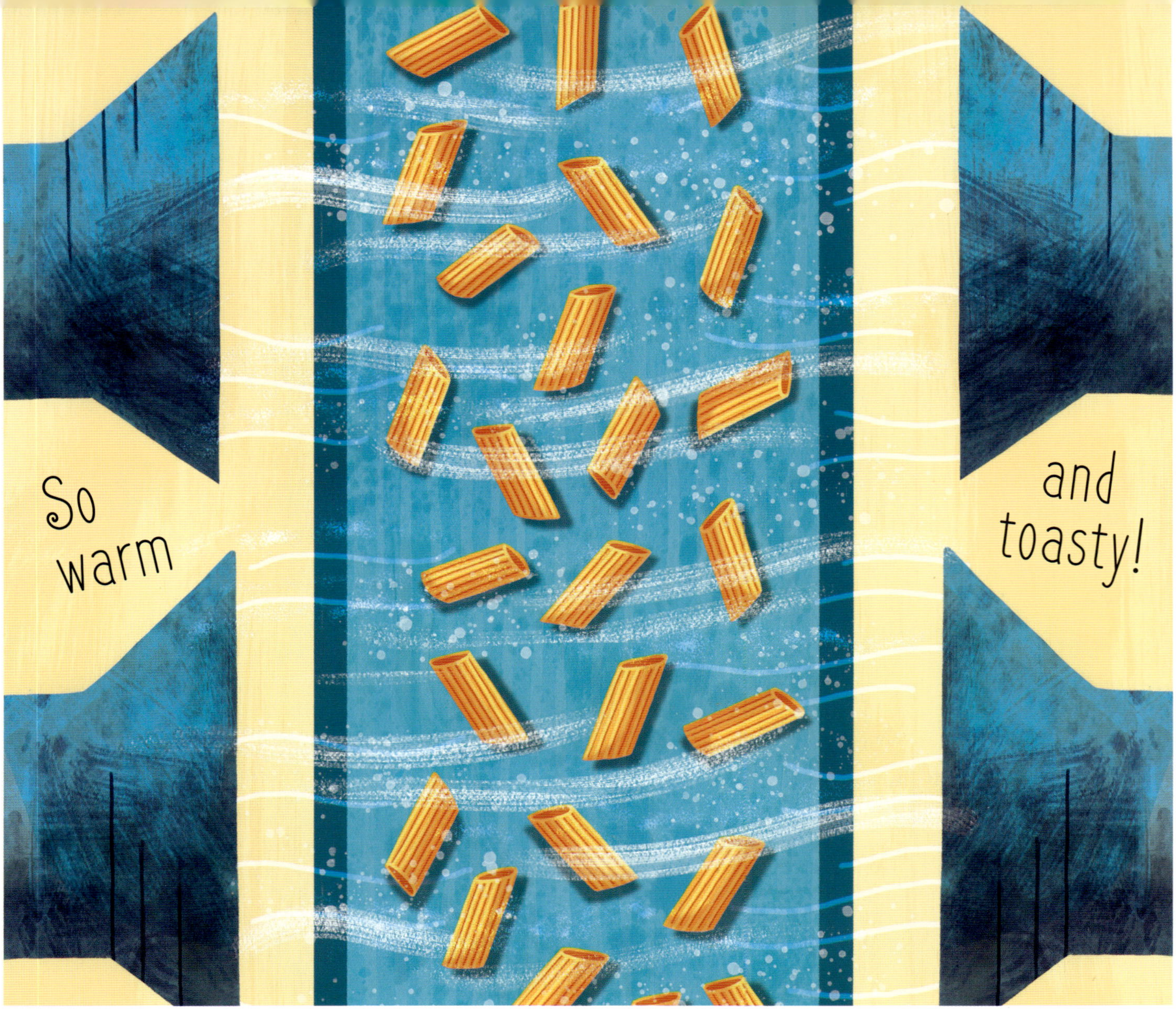

The wet pasta travels on conveyor belts. Dryers dry the pasta. Be careful. Drying pasta for too long can make it crack.

Check the dried pasta. Then package it and ship it to stores for people to enjoy.

Thanks to the wheat farmers, mill workers, and pasta factory workers, you have a delicious bowl of pasta for lunch. Yum!

WHERE IS DURUM WHEAT GROWN?

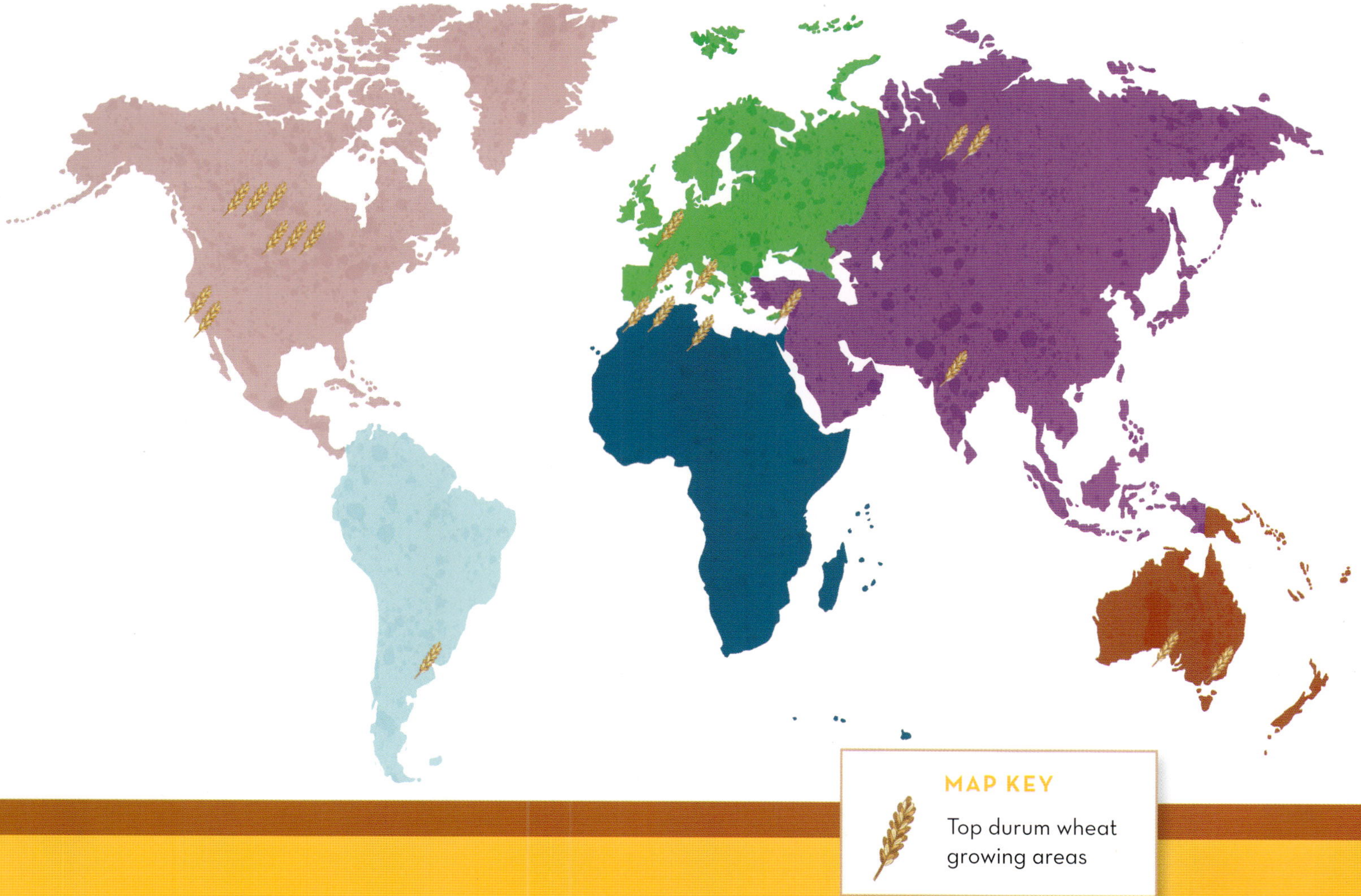

GLOSSARY

amber A dark orange-yellow color.

coarse Having a rough texture.

combine A machine that harvests wheat by cutting it, separating the kernel from the rest of the plant.

extruder A machine that shapes pasta by forcing it through special holes.

hopper The part of a combine where grain is stored.

kernel The part of the wheat plant that is used to make flour.

semolina A coarse flour that is made by grinding the endosperm of durum wheat.

silo A tall, round tower used to store crops after harvest.

WEBSITES

Beano.com: Pasta Facts
https://www.beano.com/posts/pasta-facts
Learn all sorts of pasta facts.

Kids Cyber: Pasta
https://www.kidcyber.com.au/pasta
Learn about durum wheat and the history of pasta.

PBS: Kids Vision: Pasta Factory
https://pbslearningmedia.org/resource/221a917a-dced-4cbe-8941-022395899700e/kidvision-pasta-factory/
Visit a pasta factory to see how pasta is made.

Every effort has been made to ensure that these websites are appropriate for children. However, because of the nature of the Internet, it is impossible to guarantee that these sites will remain active indefinitely or that their contents will not be altered.

READ MORE

Leaf, Christina. *Macaroni & Cheese.* Minneapolis: Bellwether Media, 2020.

Nelson, Penelope S. *Spaghetti.* Minneapolis: Cody Koala, and imprint of Pop!, 2019.

Nieminen, Lotta. *Spaghetti!: An Interactive Recipe Book.* New York: Phaidon Press, 2023.